# Superhuman Leadership NOW!

## Leadership

### How To Be Confident And Charismatic, Build Rapport And Workplace Morale, Lead And Influence People With Communication Skills, Body Language And More!

**Mick McPherson**

**STOP!!! Before you read any further....Would you like to know the Secrets of Transforming your life, overcome insecurities, develop leadership skills, and undeniable confidence in your personal, professional, and relationship life?**

If your answer is yes, then you are not alone. Thousands of people are looking for the secret to have unstoppable confidence and self-driven power in all areas of their lives.

If you have been searching for these answers without much luck, you're in the right place!

Not only will you gain incredible insight in this book, but because I want to make sure to give you as much value as possible, right now for a limited time you can get full **100% FREE access to a VIP bonus EBook** entitled **LIMITLESS ENERGY!**

**Just Go Here For Free Instant Access:**

**www.PotentialRise.com**

# Legal Notice

# Disclaimer Notice

information contained herein on the new conditions whenever they see applicable.

# Table Of Contents

# Introduction

I want to thank you and congratulate you for purchasing the book, *"Leadership: Superhuman Leadership NOW! - How To Be Confident And Charismatic, Build Rapport And Workplace Morale, Lead And Influence People With Communication Skills, Body Language And More!"*.

Leadership Superhuman Guide!

This leadership book contains proven steps and strategies on how to quickly, efficiently, and dramatically enhance your leadership skills and others willingness to follow you and your vision. If you are tired of not receiving the respect you feel you should be given, or you just want to turn yourself into a world class leader and visionary, then this book is for you!

There are a lot of things that a good leader should be. Aside from excelling in his or her field of choice, it is just as important to have excellent interpersonal skills and high emotional quotient in order to deal with people of different personalities. Being persuasive, confident, and flexible are some other traits that a good leader should possess.

This book provides techniques and courses of action for anyone wishing to become a superhuman leader. I hope you take the time to read through the chapters and integrate the insights you've gained into your day-to-day affairs.

Thanks again for purchasing this book, I hope you enjoy it!

# Chapter 1: Examples Of Ordinary People Who Became Superhuman Leaders!

Have you heard the catchphrase, "Everyone needs a hero"? It's true. People need someone to look up to and serve as an inspiration. For many of us, this hero comes in the form of a well-regarded and well-known leader.

But even the best leaders do not necessarily start out as extraordinary right off the bat – far from it. In fact, the most inspiring superhuman leaders are those who managed to overcome the challenges and obstacles along their way on their quest to become better leaders. "From zero to hero" is probably one way of describing their journey.

Here are a few examples of ordinary people who rose from relative obscurity to become some of the most exemplary leaders we know today:

- Steve Jobs

When it comes to iconic figures, Steve Jobs is definitely up there as one of the most influential leaders in the information technology sector. Best known for his role in catapulting Apple to global prominence via the iPod, iPhone, and iPad range of products, Jobs was esteemed for clean product aesthetics and visionary marketing approaches.

But all his wealth and prominence later in life was actually the sum of all the hardships he had to endure as a child. Put up for adoption by his biological parents, he grew up with little means. In fact, he had to drop out of college because his adopted parents couldn't afford his college studies anymore. Such challenges only served to drive up Jobs' motivation to succeed and be the best in his field.

- Steven Spielberg

When it comes to blockbuster Hollywood movies, one of the most prominent names that comes to mind is Steven Spielberg. The director of a number of notable classics, such as "ET" and "Jurassic Park", among countless others, Spielberg typifies the creativity and hard work that come with creating movies.

But Spielberg is an anomaly in the film industry. Prior to becoming an award-winning leader in Hollywood filmmaking, he was a teen dreamer whose desire of becoming a filmmaker was dashed when he was rejected by his dream school in college. But far from getting distraught, Spielberg ended up spinning his own happy ending.

- Angela Merkel

Currently the chancellor of Germany, Angela Merkel has been named many times over as the world's most powerful woman. She is the first woman to occupy such a sensitive post, which has seen her overseeing Europe's biggest economy amidst a sea of economic and political crises. But did you know that Merkel started out as a researcher at a laboratory?

- Mark Zuckerberg

Mark Zuckerberg is an example of a whiz college dropout from Harvard whose programming skills were put to good use in creating what is now the largest and most successful social media site to date. A relative unknown back in the day, he now sits on top of a multibillion dollar enterprise that has made him a global leader in web communications at a very young age.

Do you want to become a superhuman leader yourself? First off, you need to develop your charisma. The next chapter provides details on how you can be charismatic yourself.

# Chapter 2: How To Be Confident And Charismatic - The Secret Weapon Of Great Leaders

Charisma is a trait that can be very difficult to point out in concrete terms, but one that is immediately apparent to someone who has it. Most people can identify whether a person is charismatic or not by just a single look. Many prominent people have it. In fact, it is arguable whether or not their charisma played a key role in bringing them to where they are now.

For leaders, having charisma can be an invaluable trait. Simply put, charisma refers to the natural ability to draw people in. It is akin to having a captivating or magnetic personality. When used properly, being charismatic can lead to a lot of opportunities.

It is different from confidence, although being confident plays a key role in having charisma. So the question is: can charisma be developed, and if so, how?

Here are a few pointers to help you be more charismatic as a leader:

- Be engaging

Do not be a wallflower, respond to people, and engage in small talk. Be interesting without going overboard. Being engaging means you are able to communicate well and can properly adjust with whatever personality you come across.

- Mind your body language

It is important that you project a sense of confidence that is not intimidating, as if everyone is beneath you – far from it. There must be a clear signal or power and authority because people are naturally attracted to people who assert their dominance in a sea of mediocrity.

- Look straight in the eye

Show that you are sincere and actively listening by maintaining eye contact. Shifty eyes are usually associated with people who are lying or who can't be trusted. However, there's a thin line between maintaining an eye contact and being creepy by staring for far too long than is otherwise necessary, so learn to balance things out.

- Be a good listener and make the person you are talking to feel special.

Even though people with charisma often have everybody's attention, they also have a peculiar skill of making others feel good about themselves. Admittedly, this is a deft skill that takes time to master, but listening, empathizing, and acknowledging others are usually enough to make others feel valued.

- Use humor

You do not have to be too serious all the time. Learn to have a good laugh with others. You can be self-deprecating too, if needed. Have fun and do not take yourself too seriously. Life is not an exam, so lighten up and make the world a happy place to live in.

Know that developing charisma takes time. It doesn't happen overnight. Begin by practicing confidence. With continued practice, it should come naturally. Do not try too hard; doing so will only make you look desperate and needy, which is exactly the opposite of being charismatic.

# Chapter 3: Power Building Rapport Strategies For Getting People To Follow You And Your Vision

Starting a conversation with someone you don't know can be a very stressful experience. Most people bring books, wear headphones, or distract themselves with other things just so they can avoid having to talk with other people.

However, building rapport with others has its own benefits. When you build rapport, you actually get to expand your social circle, learn new things, and possibly beef up your network of contacts. In other words, there is really nothing to lose if you take some time out and get to know other people.

The most challenging part about building rapport is in how to start it. The art of making small talk is dependent on a lot of things, such as the body language of the other party, the place, the time, and the occasion. However, there are a number of things that can be considered universal when initiating small talk.

### *Common ground*

Chief among these things is the need to find a common ground. What exactly are you going to talk about with someone you just met? Many people suggest to bring up the weather, which is a cliché but can be a really effective launching pad for other topics.

To make it easier, learn to be observant. Look at the place around you. Listen to the music or sound in the background. Note the food being served, or the type of people around. Take cues from your immediate environment.

Once you've breached the initial barrier, just learn to enjoy the conversation and go with the flow. From a general topic, you can narrow it down to more specific ones. As you do so, be respectful and gauge if you are already sounding intrusive. In small talks, the key is not to force the other person to provide the information you need; such information must be willingly volunteered without you asking.

### *Displaying empathy*

Another crucial element is the need to show empathy. Listen to what the other person is saying and respond appropriately. At the same time, take note of the small things, such as rate of speech, mannerisms, the way the other person talks and pronounces words, and adjust accordingly. Use humor to lighten up the mood.

When done right, building rapport can lead to friendships and possibly some contacts that you can talk to again in the future.

# Chapter 4: Tips For Increasing Workplace Morale, Or Morale Of Any Organization In Minutes And Enhancing Your Team Building Efforts

The workplace can be very stressful sometimes. In between deadlines and various other projects, members of your staff can get worn out, or worse, lose motivation to keep going. This is perfectly normal because people can only endure so much. But this doesn't mean that you can't do anything to spring morale back into your workforce.

Here are a few easy suggestions that you can use the next time your workplace needs a little motivation:

- Acknowledge accomplishments

People just don't work for the sake of working. Some do so because they are passionate about what they do, while others are keen on learning new things to enrich their knowledge and skills. So it definitely helps to make it a policy to acknowledge accomplishments at work. Not only will this make your employees feel good about themselves, it also serves as a validation of their hard work and their value in the organization.

- Provide incentives and perks

While verbal recognition is helpful, make it more fun by providing additional incentives and perks in the form of cash rewards, paid vacations, or gift certificates. Having a tangible proof of their hard work makes employees more motivated and feel appreciated.

- Go out as a team

Every once in a while, go out as a team. Grab some drinks or maybe sing at a karaoke bar. Doing this will strengthen friendships and give them a breather from their usual tasks at the office.

- Have free food at the office

This is particularly helpful when everybody is deeply buried in work because of a looming deadline. But even when there is no deadline, having food at the office and having everyone partake in the feast is a good way to foster bonding and lighten the mood.

- Sponsor community service outside of the workplace

Nothing makes people feel good about themselves other than the chance to provide a part of their time helping others. And when people feel good about themselves, the better they become at what they do.

And finally, foster open communication. Know what your employees think about. You can do this by having a suggestion box or employing a feedback mechanism that will allow them to voice out their thoughts or opinions about anything at work.

This will also give you the opportunity to be clued in on office-related issues and step in if necessary to solve the problem. Similarly, this is a great way to identify the steps you need to take in order to make the workplace better and less toxic.

# Chapter 5: Techniques For Developing World Class Communication Skills When Speaking In Large Or Small Groups

To be an effective leader, you must be persuasive enough to convince your troops to rally behind your cause. One way of doing this is by being able to communicate well, not only with one or two people at a time, but also with a large group, if necessary. This can be particularly daunting. In fact, many people hold a profound fear of speaking in public. But as a leader, this is a fear that you should be able to overcome or at least learn to deal with.

Part of the reason why many people are scared of speaking before an audience is because their inherent fears precede the actual speech. Fear of making a fool of themselves, mispronouncing words, bumbling on stage, or being a bore get the better of them, much so that they lose interest in going up the stage altogether. Thankfully there are a couple of effective ways that you can subscribe to in order to ensure that you come across as a world-class communicator.

### *Know your audience*

The first rule is to always get to know who you will be talking to. You should be aware of who your audience is going to be. Doing so allows you to formulate the right approach in getting your message across. A presentation at a boardroom full of C-level executives obviously warrants a different approach as opposed to a meeting with rank-and-file employees.

Similarly, be familiar with where you will be talking at. This is particularly useful if it's your first time to talk at a certain venue. If possible, inspect the place before your actual talk. Walk up the stage, go to the podium. Get yourself comfortable with the venue. This helps in easing up tension.

When you are on the stage talking, remember that you are not there talking to yourself. Make attempts to connect with your audience. Use humor, anecdotes, trivia, or anything that will drive home your point without you being too technical or academic.

## *Project confidence*

At the same time, mind your posture. You want to have a straight back, and you want to minimize the movement of your hands or any other unnecessary gestures that only serve to distract your audience. Studies show that observing proper posture increases your confidence, so try not to slouch.

If worst comes to worst, practice basic relaxation techniques. Do not let your fears overrun your delivery of your speech. Practice deep breathing to slow down your heart rate and make you less fidgety. Before coming up the stage, you can also try yoga or meditation to clear your mind from stress or any other unwanted thoughts.

And lastly, nothing beats constant practice. Even the best public speakers take some time out to perfect their craft by practicing and keeping at it until they are confident enough to deliver it before hundreds or even thousands of listeners. The same is true in your case. The more you take the time to hone your communication skills, the better you become.

# Chapter 6: Understanding The Role Body Language Plays And How People Perceive You Based On Your Nonverbal Communication

A lot can be gleamed from a person on account of how he or she moves or responds to things even if he or he is not saying anything. This is nonverbal language at work. It is instinctive for humans to be particularly sensitive about these things. In fact, studies show that people respond better to another person's actions rather than his or her words. As a leader, it is therefore necessary that you are able to project what you want to show through the use of nonverbal communication.

Because of the rather heavy focus put on speech or choice of words, nonverbal communication is often not tackled as frequently as it should. The result? There is generally a mismatch between what you are saying and what your body language is suggesting.

If you are trying to project confidence and authority, even the little things count. Begin with the handshake. A firm and solid grip is often associated with someone who is confident and secure, whereas a weak grip is taken to mean as a sign of uncertainty or insecurity.

### Inspiring confidence

Your posture is also generally used as an indication of how you are feeling or doing at this moment. If you are slouching, it usually means you are either tired or bored. On the contrary, observing proper posture not only makes you look confident, it also makes you feel more confident. Proper posture is associated with power and authority, so having a straight back inspires confidence in other people.

Another way to inspire confidence is by smiling. A simple smile can be a doorway for many opportunities. It suggests that you are accommodating, willing to listen, and friendly. As such, many people would be willing to talk with you than to someone who hardly smiles.

And finally, do away with physical obstructions between you and other people. When you set a boundary between yourself and others, you are in effect saying that you are unwelcoming. For example, if you close your office's door, that is a clear indication that nobody is supposed to come in. Essentially, you are blocking out everyone else.

This is precisely the reason why many professionals now choose to implement an open door policy to assure their staff that they are welcome to talk to them anytime. Having an open door policy provides an assurance to everyone that they matter and that they have an opportunity to be heard anytime.

# Chapter 7: Leading By Example By Showing Your Commitment To Time Management And Excellence

Just how important is time to you as a leader? Do you thrive under pressure or are you able to work better when given enough time to prepare? Is your regard for time notable enough for your followers to take notice?

It begins with the most basic things. For example, always clocking in at work early will easily dissuade the rest from clocking in at a later time. Poor appreciation of time by leaders inevitably results in other people imitating their lead. After all, if a leader does it, then everyone will, too.

But beyond coming in for work on time – which, when you think about it, is actually a professional obligation – it is crucial that the leader presents time as a valuable element in achieving the organization's goals. As a leader, you should be keenly aware of just how vital time is in the overall scheme of things, and how it is equally vital for everyone else to cooperate in achieving success.

- Create goals

Before even buckling down for work, it is vital that you create a list of both short- and long-term goals. These goals will guide you in coming up with a timeline that is reasonable and realistic. In coming up with your goals, try to be as specific as possible. For example, if your ultimate goal is to successfully launch a new product, then it is much wiser to break this down into a set of short-term goals, such as doing market research, coming up with a preliminary design, creating marketing collateral, and signing up deals with retailers.

- Set reasonable and realistic deadlines

Now that you have your goals, it is time to prepare deadlines.

Without deadlines, you are basically operating with no clear output in sight anytime soon. Deadlines, while restrictive, can be used as a way to motivate others to work. But be sure that these deadlines are reasonable and realistic. Following the example above, how long will it take to launch a new product? How much time is needed to conduct market research? When will the preliminary design be made available? These things must be considered vis-à-vis the available resources, manpower, and skills of the people who are supposed to do them.

- Gauge the results

After the deadlines have passed, it is necessary that the results be gauged to assess if the desired results have been achieved. Take some time to discuss with your staff about the quality of the output, what can be done to improve it, and what the next logical course of action is going to be.

In all these, it is necessary that you display discipline, firmness, and flexibility, especially if it is warranted. Discipline is important in making sure that you and your organization do not lose track of what you set out to achieve in the first place. Firmness is needed in ensuring that everybody adheres to the agreed timetable. And lastly, you should show flexibility if the situation calls for it. Things do not go as planned sometimes, so if you are conscientious enough, you must have backup plans ready in case the original one does not pan out well.

# Chapter 8: Management Principles To Follow When Dealing With Difficult People

As a leader, it is incumbent upon you to make sure that the workplace and the people who comprise it are not only productive and efficient, but also happy with what they are doing. For many, this comes as a tall order, mainly because there is no such thing as a utopia workplace.

Consider this: no two people are exactly alike. Each worker has a personality that is distinct from the rest. And while any manager would ideally prefer a united workforce, the fact of the matter is that there will always be a few individuals who will stand out for all the wrong reasons.

Difficult people exist everywhere. The nature of their character is one where the people around them are repulsed by their behavior. Worse, their character can affect the way others work and can even serve as a legitimate detriment in achieving the organization's goals.

In your case, it is your prerogative to get equally repulsed by them, but this does not mean that you will not be doing anything to remedy the situation. As a leader, you should hold yourself accountable in learning how to deal with these sorts of people and hopefully find a real solution to the problem at hand.

So how exactly do you deal with difficult people? Here are a number of essential principles you should keep in mind:

- Develop a profound sense of self-awareness

If you find that some people you are directly dealing with are being difficult, it is better to take a moment to be introspective before launching an offensive. Take a good look at yourself and answer the following questions: Is it possible that you are the problem?

Are you doing anything that makes other people around you react in a negative manner? Have you dealt with situations like this before? Do you see a recurring pattern in the way other people deal with you?

If you answered in the affirmative to any of the questions above, then now is as good a time as any to address your own personal issues.

- Deal with the situation head on

If you are confronted with a situation where a difficult person is involved, address the situation right away. This is particularly important when the said difficult person is causing a directly observable impact on inter-office relations or causing a negative impact on the overall performance of the organization.

Remember that choosing to look the other way will not solve the problem. In fact, it may even aggravate it further. When employees, for example, feel that their leader is not doing enough to spare them from the toxicity brought about by a difficult coworker, they may develop a sense of resentment toward you.

- Maintain objectivity and a sense of control

In dealing with a difficult person, it is necessary that you do not let your emotions or biases get the better of you. It is important that you maintain a sense of objectivity because otherwise you risk appearing to be favoring one party over the other. It's a careful balancing act. This also harks back to the previous point where issues with difficult people need to be nipped in the bud while you still can because the moment they morph into something bigger and destructive, it will be particularly hard to retain your control.

- Direct confrontation is not really a good option, but it can be useful sometimes

One of the things that you should do away with is confronting difficult people in public. Doing so only serves to validate their behavior. In addition, you take the risk of provoking them into launching an emotional or physical attack, which is the last thing you would want to see in a situation like this.

That being said, there are circumstances where a public confrontation is a valid response. If constant communication and closed door discussion with the difficult person do not result in anything positive, then it's time to show a clear display of power and authority to put said difficult person in his/her right place.

- Weigh things evenly, but always have the common good at the heart of your intervention

As much as possible, be honest with the parties involved. Facilitate an open exchange of ideas on how to best resolve the situation. Use humor if it's warranted. But know that in everything you do, your primary concern should always be geared toward the common good.

Your worth both as a manager and as a leader is measured not only by the title or position you hold. More importantly, a lot of it is based on your ability to deal with all kinds of people, including the difficult ones.

The next chapter discusses in detail how to assert your authority further through your creativity and imagination.

# Chapter 9: Using Creativity To Keep Your Leadership Skills Fresh And Not Lose The Attention Of Your Followers

One of the most frequently overlooked traits that leaders must have is being creative. Part of the reason why it is not given due emphasis is because of the fact that it is hard to identify in concrete terms, and even harder to measure.   This is in stark contrast to other competencies, such as financial wizardry, which can be easily gauged using available quantitative data.

But now more than ever, creativity comes as a vital component of being a good leader. Prevailing market conditions pay a premium on novel and out-of-the-box ideas. And for the most part, while it is so much easier to stick to tried and tested formulas, being bold enough to rely on fresh ideas provides a good look at the kind of leader you are.

Creativity and innovation go hand in hand. A creative leader is not afraid to try out new models and approaches as a way of finding out if there is a better way of doing things. Whether it's drawing new business models, infusing fresh concepts to strengthen your position in the market, or crafting new policies to attract or to retain outstanding talent, creativity plays a key role in helping you meet both your personal and organizational goals.

### Not stifled by tradition

Aside from their openness to new things, creative leaders are also marked by the fact that they are not stifled by tradition. They are always on the lookout for new and untested concepts, knowing full well that although risky, the potential returns can be a great turning point for everyone involved.

Creativity can come in many forms. For example, most leaders are content in following the hierarchical management model, where everything comes down from the top and flows downward to the people of lower rank.

Creative leaders can present a new alternative by trying to draw inputs from all ranks instead of monopolizing the exchange of ideas. Doing this presents a greater opportunity for everyone to be heard. And since ideas are coming from beyond the usual sources, expect the rush of new and possibly better ideas.

Still on the subject of people, part of being creative as a leader is your ability to bring in the right kind of people to do the job. No matter how visionary you are as a leader, you still need the support of others to bring your ideas to life. In this regard, you want to be working with the best people who have the clearest potential to deliver good results.

Diversity in the inflow of thoughts and ideas, as well as diversity in the workplace provide dynamism within the organization, putting it in a constant state of growth. This kind of environment provides everyone a reason to be excited with their work, and you a chance to be a leader that people can look up to and be truly proud of.

# Chapter 10: 10 Rules To Follow To Increase Your Leadership Presence And The Confidence Others Have In You

An oft debated concept is whether leaders are made or born. The fact of the matter is everyone has the potential to become a good leader. However, only a few have what it takes to be a great leader.

You know one when you see one on account of his or her demeanor, delivery of words, appeal, and competence in delivering what is expected of him or her, often going above and beyond the usual in order to surpass expectations. These traits make great leaders good role models, and as such are looked up to by many people.

Making your presence known and convincing others to have faith in you may come naturally for a few people. For many others, however, these two require deft skills, as well as an ample sense of sensitivity and self-awareness. In this regard, here are 10 rules to follow to increase your leadership presence and the confidence others have in you:

1. Be attentive to the needs of others

A leader is not just supposed to mind his or her own needs. An essential trait that all good leaders must possess is the ability to gauge what their followers need. For it is in addressing such needs that one's leadership skills are honed and made better.

2. Be honest

Manipulating your followers by crafting lies and other dishonest statements is probably the worst thing that you can do as a leader. No matter how inconvenient the truth is, it is your responsibility as a leader to let others know what they are up to or what the state of affairs is.

3. Respect everyone

This should be a given and need not be underscored, but it's also something that many so-called leaders fail to live by. Respect comes in many forms, such as willingness to listen to others' opinions, openness to new ideas, or appreciating the hard work of other people. Respect must be accorded to everyone regardless of age, sex, religion, or rank.

4. Pay attention to how you look

This may come across as superficial, but the ways you look and handle yourself are vital in how others perceive you. As a leader, you are expected to look clean and well put together. You may have the best skills in the world, but if you look like someone that others wouldn't want to be near to, then you lose the confidence of others in you.

5. Adhere to the highest professional and moral standards

It's not just enough that you are the best in your field; it is just as important to imbibe a sense of propriety in everything you do. Otherwise, it would be difficult, if not completely impossible, to have people rally behind your back.

6. Be mindful of your mannerisms

Many leaders are unable to convince others of their worth simply because they appear weak, vulnerable, too casual, or not smart enough. Many of these are due to negative mannerisms. For example, slouching or flailing your hands too much hardly counts as reassuring. It's all about how you project yourself to your intended public. The more confident and assured you seem, the easier it is for people to believe in what you are telling them.

7. Assert authority in your voice and choice of words

Sounding unsure is the worst thing a leader can do when telling others what to do. A leader must be assertive, but not in a rambunctious or offending way. There must be a clear signal of authority emanating from your voice, your tone, and your choice of words. If you find this to be your weak spot, take some time to practice until you master the skill. After all, leadership is not just about the words you choose to utter. More than anything else, it's about how you say these words and what you do after that really count the most.

8. Be fair to everyone

Nothing ruins any organization more than the idea that the leader unjustly leans in favor of one party over the other. To succeed as a leader, you must project objectivity. It's completely impossible to get rid of your own biases, but professionalism dictates that fairness and willingness to listen to opposing sides must be displayed at all times.

9. Be visible

Do not hide or try to appear invisible. You don't need to be available 24/7 either, but at the very least, you should be present when it counts the most. A missing leader is an ineffective leader.

10. Most importantly, learn to deliver results

The most critical aspect of being a leader is when you are able to deliver what is expected of you, or maybe even more. To be a leader is to have a set of goals in mind and actually accomplishing them. These achievements may not come all at once, or it may be a long time coming before anything worthwhile comes out, but what is important is to keep struggling by learning from past misgivings and being bold enough to accept challenges along the way.

These are just some of the things that you can do to boost your leadership presence and make others feel assured of your competence as someone they look up to. As a leader, it is critical that you are able to create a sustainable balance between your technical competencies and your ability to deal with people of different personalities and backgrounds.

In the end, much is expected of you. Therefore, it is just right and proper that you equip yourself with the needed tools and mindset to ensure that your own brand of leadership results in achieving both personal and organizational goals, and in inspiring others to be at their best.

# Conclusion

Thank you again for purchasing this book on what it takes to become a great leader!

I am extremely excited to pass this information along to you, and I am so happy that you now have read and can hopefully implement these strategies going forward.

I hope this book was able to help you understand the dynamics of effective and creative leadership, as well as discover ways on how to inspire others and bring out the best in them.

The next step is to get started using this information and to hopefully live a life of commitment, understanding, and inspired leadership!

Please don't be someone who just reads this information and doesn't apply it, the strategies in this book will only benefit you if you use them!

If you know of anyone else that could benefit from the information presented here please inform them of this book.

Finally, if you enjoyed this book and feel it has added value to your life in any way, please take the time to share your thoughts and post a review on Amazon. It'd be greatly appreciated!

Thank you and good luck!

Preview Of:

*Quick Project Management For Beginners!*

# Project Management

*Influence, Lead, And Manage Your Team For Increased Productivity And Performance*

# Introduction

I want to thank you and congratulate you for purchasing the book, *"Project Management: Quick Project Management For Beginners! - Influence, Lead, And Manage Your Team For Increased Productivity And Performance!"*

This "Project Management" book contains proven steps and strategies on how to become a good project manager. This involves knowing the basics of making an effective project plan, how to manage time effectively, manage risks, monitor the performance of your team members, and different qualities that a project manager should possess.

Most organizations do not have enough time to get their employees working on projects, compelling them to rely on third party project management teams to do the job for them. This explains why the project management field is progressing these days, and why some people want to become project managers of certain teams. However, project management is not a simple task. It involves working on producing numerous outputs at any given time, managing teams that are formed solely for the project and are not really bonded together, and lastly dealing with contingencies so that the group will be able to deliver what is expected of them. This implies that if the project manager is not competent enough for the position, the project will ultimately end in failure.

With the help of this book, aspiring project managers will know the basics of the field that they want to be in and prepare for what they will be experiencing once they're managing their own project team.

Thanks again for purchasing this book. I hope you enjoy it!

# Chapter 1 - The Basics Of Project Management

Every organization has numerous tasks that should be accomplished; some tasks have longer durations, and may need to be constantly taken care of, while others are short-lived and are only introduced because the need for it arose. These short term tasks are also known as projects. But even if projects are temporary tasks that need to be carried out, it doesn't mean that they should be attended to unsystematically. There is a proper method that should be followed if you want a good outcome for the project that should be accomplished.

This chapter will discuss basic information about project management.

## Defining points of project management

In this chapter's introduction, the term project management was given a brief definition. But aside from having a general idea as to what this concept is about, it's also important that the different points surrounding project management are defined. It is only by specifying these points that we will truly understand what this concept is.

These factors are as follows:

- Project management has an exact beginning and end – projects are simply temporary tasks that the organization needs to be accomplished and delivered before the deadline. To differentiate it from regular work, projects are usually not repeatable; if ever it will have to be repeated, this usually happens after a significant amount of time has passed.

- Project management is an independent work – another difference between regular work at an organization and projects is that the former usually relies on the output of other departments, whereas the latter is independent. This simply means that even if the project team was not able to deliver the task assigned to it, other departments can carry out their work and will not affect their performance.

- Project managements utilize different tools to identify the tasks that were accomplished and the progress of the whole team compared to the time that they still have – in order for project managers to determine if they are on the right track and if they can accomplish the said task within the specified time frame, they use different tools to measure success. Some of these tools are Gantt and PERT charts, and a Work Breakdown table that is based on the objectives created before the project starts.

- Project management increases the probability of a task to turn out as successful – project managers look at all angles to determine the risks and possible problems that they may experience while doing the task. This will obviously result in devising a good plan so that the objectives can be met and the task will be delivered successfully.

## Three factors for successful project management

For project management to become successful, there are three general factors that every team should consider:

- Time – as mentioned, projects follow a specified schedule and should be delivered before that deadline comes. Otherwise, the outcome of the project may be unused.

- Scope – the project should follow certain boundaries so that the outcome is specialized for the department or organization that requested for the task. For example, if you are asked to provide an architectural blueprint for a commercial building, make sure that the end product will not look like something else.

- Cost – just like time, most projects have a certain budget to cover the expenses needed for its accomplishment. All project managers strive to deliver the project successfully while using the least amount of resources.

Now that you have learned about the definition of project management and what factors should be present in order for it to become successful, the focus will now be shifted to the actual process of project management.

# Thanks for Previewing My Exciting Book Entitled:

## "Project Management: Influence, Lead, And Manage Your Team For Increased Productivity And Performance"

To purchase this book, simply go to the Amazon Kindle store and simply search:

"PROJECT MANAGEMENT"

Then just scroll down until you see my book. You will know it is mine because you will see my name "Mick McPherson" underneath the title.

Alternatively, you can visit my author page on Amazon to see this book and other work I have done. Thanks so much, and please don't forget your free bonuses

**DON'T LEAVE YET! - CHECK OUT YOUR FREE BONUSES BELOW!**

# Free Bonus Offer: Get Free Access To The PotentialRise.com VIP Newsletter!

Once you enter your email address you will immediately get free access to this awesome newsletter!

But wait, right now if you join now for free you will also get free access to the "LIMITLESS ENERGY" free EBook!

To claim both your FREE VIP NEWSLETTER MEMBERSHIP and your FREE BONUS Ebook on LIMITLESS ENERGY!

Just Go To:

## www.PotentialRise.com

www.ingramcontent.com/pod-product-compliance
Lightning Source LLC
Chambersburg PA
CBHW071551170526
45166CB00004B/1636